Grizzled Bill
Turns Over a New Leaf

by Jason Lublinski ♦ illustrated by Sean O'Neill

Editorial Offices: Glenview, Illinois • Parsippany, New Jersey • New York, New York
Sales Offices: Needham, Massachusetts • Duluth, Georgia • Glenview, Illinois
Coppell, Texas • Ontario, California • Mesa, Arizona

Every effort has been made to secure permission and provide appropriate credit for photographic material. The publisher deeply regrets any omission and pledges to correct errors called to its attention in subsequent editions.

Unless otherwise acknowledged, all photographs are the property of Scott Foresman, a division of Pearson Education.

ISBN: 0-328-13645-X

Copyright © Pearson Education, Inc.

All Rights Reserved. Printed in the United States of America. This publication is protected by Copyright, and permission should be obtained from the publisher prior to any prohibited reproduction, storage in a retrieval system, or transmission in any form by any means, electronic, mechanical, photocopying, recording, or likewise. For information regarding permission(s), write to: Permissions Department, Scott Foresman, 1900 East Lake Avenue, Glenview, Illinois 60025.

8 9 10 V054 14 13 12 11 10 09

CONTENTS

CHAPTER 1   4
A Legend in His Own Time

CHAPTER 2   9
An Outlaw's Intentions

CHAPTER 3   14
Changing Horses Midstream

CHAPTER 4   20
A Second Chance

CHAPTER 5   26
A Brand-New Bill

A BRIEF HISTORY OF TEXAS   30

Chapter 1
A Legend in His Own Time

I first met Grizzled Bill Jones in the summer of 1865. That was a long time ago, but I remember our first meeting as though it were yesterday. To encounter him was to remember him, to say the least. I was just a teenaged ranch hand at the time, doing my best to keep an eye on the boss's cattle. But Grizzled Bill was a legend.

Stories were told about his superhuman speed and strength. It was said he could lift a horse right off the ground. His skill with a six-shooter was also the stuff of legends; he was known far and wide for his quick draw and dead-on aim. But Grizzled Bill had never killed a man.

The common folk didn't think he was a villain like other outlaws. That's because the rugged, gray-bearded man was something of a cowboy Robin Hood.

When Grizzled Bill stole from rich Texas landowners, he would give some or all of his loot to the needy. This earned him a sizeable group of admirers, even if they had doubts about his methods. For life in Texas cattle country was no easy road for ordinary people. The rich cattle barons pretty much did as they pleased. They even used us in their little wars against each other. So it was comforting to believe that we had someone on our side.

We all dreamed of crossing paths with the illustrious Grizzled Bill Jones. But on July 5, 1865, in Asparosa, Texas, my dream came true.

★ ★ ★ ★ ★

First let me tell you a little about myself. My name is Sam Granite. On that fateful day in 1865, I was eighteen years old, working as a cowboy on the Triple J Ranch. The Triple J was huge and highly profitable, with more cattle than I'd ever seen.

The Triple J's owner was Curtis Clay Wilkinson, an arrogant man. I was his newest hire, one of a team of ten men who were responsible for the northern quarter of the ranch. Three other teams took care of the eastern, western, and southern parts. So Wilkinson had himself a small army of cowboys. He loved having a huge troop of men to order around at his leisure.

I was not fond of my employer. But there was little I could do about it. I was educated, but I was from a poor family. Working at the Triple J was supposed to be one of the best jobs around. That's because you got room and board and three square meals a day.

I lived in a big wooden building with the other nine cowhands from my team. We slept in one long room, shared an outhouse, and ate in the mess hall with the other ranch hands.

We worked six days a week, from five in the morning to well after dark. Lights-out was at eleven. It was as if we were in bondage, forced to do whatever Mr. Wilkinson wanted. I missed my family. I missed my girlfriend, Eloise. I hated never having enough time to read. Mr. Wilkinson drove us all hard: any problem, we had to work until it was fixed.

I planned to work at the Triple J for five years, enough time to save enough money to go to college in the East. Then Eloise and I would get married and start a new life far from Texas. Escape: that's what I dreamed of.

Everything changed when I met Grizzled Bill.

* * * * *

I was out one afternoon, inspecting the Triple J's north fence, when a dark rider came galloping up. I was suspicious immediately. The stranger was large, gray-bearded and tough-looking.

"Afternoon," I said, cautiously.

"You work here?" the rider said in a laid-back drawl.

"Yep," I said. "But I'm gonna have to ask you to leave. This here is private property."

I was doing my best to sound firm. But in truth, I was trembling inside. I had no idea who this lone rider was, but he looked big and mean.

"I know it's private property," he said. "It's the Triple J Ranch, isn't it? Belongs to a man called Curtis Clay Wilkinson?"

"You got it right, mister, but you still need to leave," I said, trying to calm my shaky voice.

The stranger smiled. "Don't worry, young 'un," he said. "I'll leave shortly. I won't give you any trouble, either. But, first, answer this: You like working for Mr. Wilkinson?"

I was struck by the question. It wasn't what I'd expected. Just then, the wind picked up.

"Course you don't have to answer," said the rider, "But I'd appreciate it if you would."

Chapter 2
An Outlaw's Intentions

I paused for a long moment. I finally said, "No. Can't say I like working for Mr. Wilkinson. Truth be told, he's not a very kind man."

"A boss doesn't have to be a kind man, now, does he?" asked the stranger, tipping his hat back. In the sun, his face looked friendlier.

"But he don't have to be mean," I replied. "Mr. Wilkinson treats his men like dirt, just because he can. He works us awful hard. Fifteen hours a day, six days a week."

"Well, you must get paid for it," said the rider.

"I guess," I said. "I mean we get decent pay. And the food is good."

"So I've heard," he smiled.

"But I suspect he could pay a little bit more, for all the work we do," I blurted out.

I realized with dismay that I had said much more than I meant to. But once I started talking about Mr. Wilkinson and his callous ways, I just got carried away. It made me wonder what it was about this man that made me talk so much. And why would he be interested in Mr. Wilkinson?

"Can't imagine what a difference all this would make to you, mister," I said to the stranger. Nearby, my horse stamped his foot and whinnied, as if he agreed with me.

The stranger smiled. "Actually," he said, "it makes all the difference in the world. You, my young friend, just helped me decide my next feat."

"Feat?" I said, having no idea what he meant.

"See," he said, "I've heard a lot about your Mr. Wilkinson. Most of it's not very pleasant, I'm afraid. But I always make allowances for idle gossip, rumors, and speculation. When a man is a success, it can cause some tongues to wag. People might get resentful. They might feel a need to talk behind his back. I wanted to find out from someone who would know. Someone who's had first-hand dealings with the man."

"Someone like me," I said, suddenly understanding his point. I looked up at the sky. Soon the sun would be going down. The stranger was looking past me, down the hills to where Wilkinson's cattle grazed. He had an odd smile on his face.

As I studied him, the stranger realized my discomfort. "You're probably wondering who the heck I am," he said. He raised his ten-gallon hat in a salute. "Name's Grizzled Bill Jones," he said. "And I've just decided to rob your boss."

The outlaw, Grizzled Bill! And just like that, I fainted dead away.

★ ★ ★ ★ ★

I came to a few minutes later. Grizzled Bill was splashing cold water on my face. "Welcome back to the land of the living, boy," he said.

"I've heard stories about you, Mr. Grizzled Bill," I said, still feeling dizzy.

"Call me Bill," said the infamous outlaw.

"Never mind that!" I shouted. "I've heard about you! You're a robber! A thief!"

"Guilty as charged," Grizzled Bill calmly admitted. "Yep, can't deny it. But some folks seem to think I'm something of a hero."

"Well, I ain't one," I said, backing up.

Truth be told, I did think Grizzled Bill was something of a hero. I was just scared upon actually meeting him face to face. Next morning, though, I went back to mend that north fence, and there he was.

"Hungry?" he said, offering me a hunk of dried buffalo meat. "Always keep some handy," he said. "Man gets hungry out here."

I took a piece. It tasted good—better that what they served down in the mess hall.

"Ain't you never heard me referred to as the 'Robin Hood of the West'?" asked Grizzled Bill. He seemed to like the moniker.

"Never," I lied.

"I can tell you're prevaricating, boy," Bill said with a grin. "It's written all over your face."

I admitted I was.

"But you're not going to tell Old Man Wilkinson about me, are you?" he said. Now he looked serious. "Take your time before you tell me the truth."

I chewed for a moment. "Don't think so," I finally said.

We sat there for a while, Grizzled Bill gazing down the valley toward Mr. Wilkinson's house and buildings. I knew I still had a whole line of fence to fix, and time wasn't sitting still. But I didn't feel like working.

"So what exactly are you planning to do to my boss?" I said after a spell. I thought I had a right to ask.

Grizzled Bill shifted a little and took out a penknife and a stick. He began to whittle the bark off. I had to notice it was a very sharp knife.

"Nothing bad," he said. "Just raid his treasury."

"Raid his treasury!" I shouted, almost choking on my buffalo meat. "That's crazy!"

He looked up and grinned at me. "And what is so crazy about it?" he said.

"Have you ever seen his treasury? It's a huge stone building, right next to the Big House where he lives with his wife and daughter, Helga. It's guarded day and night. Five armed guards each shift."

"I see," said the outlaw.

"You'll get shot," I said. "Sure as I'm sitting here."

Bill squinted as the sun hit his face. But he didn't look too worried.

Chapter 3
Changing Horses Midstream

In the days to come, I repaired the fence and talked to Grizzled Bill. He'd come galloping up on his ebony horse, all fired up about robbing Wilkinson. But I was determined to stop him. It wasn't that I wanted to spare Wilkinson any trouble. It's just that I was beginning to like this gray-bearded outlaw who didn't really talk or act like an outlaw at all. And since I hadn't had a chance to make many friends at the ranch, it was nice to talk to him.

"Tell me what's in the treasury again," Bill said. "There's a lot of needy people just a town away."

I argued with him. "Doesn't matter," I said. No amount of gold was worth risking his life.

"Truly?" Bill said. "I'll tell you something. I haven't done any phenomenal feats in too long. I need something to keep up my reputation."

"That's no reason," I said.

Bill scratched his head. "People need me," he said.

"You don't need to steal to help people," I said. "And a crime is a crime, regardless of your reasons for committing it."

"You sound like a preacher," Bill said, sounding slightly annoyed. "You going to try something silly, like stopping me?"

We argued for what seemed like hours. "You do get caught by Mr. Wilkinson, he'll hang you for certain," I said.

"Tell me another way I can get that much money to give away to the poor," he said.

I was getting tired of this. And part of me wondered, what outlaw would spend so much time discussing the fine points of his next heist? I began to sense that there was another side to this guy. After all, he kept lumps of sugar for his horse.

"A job," I finally said.

"I've *got* a job," he said. "I like my job. I'm good at it!"

"But you're breaking the law!" I shouted in frustration.

"You noticed?" he said with a chuckle.

"You may find it funny, but I don't," I said. "You think that just because people admire you, they approve of what you're doing."

"Are you saying they don't?" asked Grizzled Bill, dumbstruck.

"People admire you because they know you have a good heart. It's clear from what you do with your ill-gotten loot. But, at the same time, people dislike that you use such nefarious means to accomplish your worthy ends."

"Really?" asked Grizzled Bill. He was starting to sound a bit unsure of himself.

"Look," I said, "maybe it's time for something else. Let's go down to Heiferville. It has a general store, post office, and saloon. Maybe we could get you a job there."

"I don't know," said Grizzled Bill, sounding nervous. "I've been an outlaw most of my life. But the idea of not having to run so hard—to actually grow old—now that's got a ring to it."

★ ★ ★ ★ ★

Sunday, my day off, we met in the Heiferville town square.

Grizzled Bill looked different. He'd gotten a haircut and trimmed his gray beard. He wore a nice jacket and had cleaned off his hat.

A young, pretty woman in glasses walked by. "Ma'am," I said, "wouldn't you say my friend here looks very dapper in his Sunday best?"

The young woman took a measured look, then smiled. "Very dapper indeed," she said.

"Never guess he was a notorious outlaw, would you?" I asked, happily.

A look of horror crossed her face. She gathered up her skirts and scurried away.

"Maybe you shouldn't tell people that part," Grizzled Bill muttered, looking downcast.

We then dropped in on Horace Mackey, proprietor of the Heiferville General Store.

"Why, hello, Sam!" he said, shaking my hand. "Good to see you! Is this the friend in need of employment?" He shook hands with Grizzled Bill as well.

"Pleased to meet you, sir," said Grizzled Bill. "My name is Bill, er, Hermitcrab."

"Any experience?" said Horace.

"Oh yes," said Bill. "Lots."

"So," said Horace, encouraged, "you've worked in general stores before?"

"Well, no, not as such," admitted Grizzled Bill. "But I've robbed them—plenty of times!"

✶ ✶ ✶ ✶ ✶

"We should probably leave the 'robbery' part out next time," I said a few minutes later, after Horace had shown us the door.

Bill looked discouraged. "Sorry about that. Guess I'm not used to this whole honest-citizen thing."

"Don't worry," I said. "It'll grow on you."

We decided to go for a root beer, just to pick up our spirits. Albert Tweezers ran the local saloon next door, and he had a fine piano.

"I could use a good piano player," Albert waited, as Bill sat down to play. To my surprise, he tickled the ivories like no other player I had ever heard. He played loudly and so fast that it sounded like four pianos, not one.

"Maybe not a saloon type of music," Albert waited politely when Grizzled Bill was done. "But for some reason, it sounds familiar." Needless to say, we hightailed it out of there. Then Bill admitted he'd spent a great deal of time in that saloon one summer, waiting to rob the local bank.

This was not going to be easy, I thought.

Chapter 4
A Second Chance

I had assumed the difficult part would be getting Grizzled Bill to give up his life of crime. Instead, the problem was that no one seemed ready to give him a chance to make an honest living. Even without really knowing him, each potential employer rejected him. They seemed to base their dislike on the most minute details.

"I warned you," said Grizzled Bill, sadly. "I told you robbery is my vocation."

"I refuse to believe that," I said. It was three Sundays later, though, and now even I was beginning to wonder. Mr. Hazel, the apothecary, didn't need anyone else to work at his drugstore. Mr. Klostermann didn't need any more stable hands at his livery barn. Mr. Barnes didn't need anyone else to sell his books. Not even the librarian, Edith Applesauce, needed help.

"I don't know what to say," I told Grizzled Bill at the end of the day.

"Don't worry, Sam," he said, reassuringly patting my shoulder. "It's not your fault."

"Yes, it is!" I said, angrily. "I'm the one who told you to quit your life of crime! I'm a dreadful adviser!"

"Actually, for a young cowpoke, you're a pretty good man," said Grizzled Bill. "Not your fault that nobody wants to hire me. But it does prove a point. A horse can't change its color."

I'd given up attempting to find Bill a job and was just trying to keep my own with Old Mean Wilkinson. Bill had disappeared for a while. I assumed he was back to robbing someone, but it wasn't Wilkinson. Then, one day, he showed up on the hill where I was mending another fence. It was already getting cold. I was thinking about my Eloise and what she must be doing. At first I didn't recognize Bill, except for his black horse.

"Hey," he called as he came galloping up. "I figured out what to do!"

"Howdy stranger," I said. "Another feat?"

I was a bit surprised when he shook his head. "Can't go back to that after what you helped me see," he said. "Matter of fact, I realized I've got to make amends for what I did."

His tone of voice sent shivers down my spine. What was he thinking?

"I'm headed to the sheriff's," he said. "Just wanted to say goodbye and thanks to you. It's taken me a month, but now I'm sure. I'm going to turn myself in. You showed me the error of my ways."

"You can't do that!" I yelled. "You're a good man now! You've changed! There's no reason to rot in jail now."

"I've made up my mind," he said, and with that, he whirled his horse around and headed for Heiferville. I couldn't let him do it. I jumped on my own horse and ran after him. "Stop!" I yelled. "You've got your whole life ahead of you!"

But he wasn't listening. Down the valley we went, raising all the dust in Texas. I chased Bill all the way into Heiferville, where we both came to a sliding stop in front of the sheriff's office. And that, my friends, is when fate stepped in.

★ ★ ★ ★ ★

I was trying to keep Bill from going in the sheriff's office when to both of our surprise, a man came bursting out of the door. He was wearing a dark suit and a bowler, and he had a big, somewhat silly-looking mustache. But he was carrying a revolver. And the sheriff was right behind him.

"Stop him!" the elderly Sheriff Abernathy shouted, between gasps for breath. "Stop, that thief!"

Before I could even think of what to do, Grizzled Bill leaped into action. The thief was about to round the corner when, as if from out of nowhere, a spur zinged through the air. It caught the thief square in the head, knocking him down. Bill was already sprinting in his direction. By the time the thief was sitting up again, shaking his head, Bill jumped on him.

"My good sir," said Sheriff Abernathy, panting as he caught up. He was red-faced and wheezing. "Why that's the most infamous thief in Oklahoma you just stopped."

"Who?" Bill said, looking at the man. I could sense a hint of wounded pride in his voice—most infamous thief, indeed!

"My utmost thanks," said the sheriff, extending his hand.

"It was nothing," said Grizzled Bill.

"It was far from nothing," said the sheriff as he led the thief toward the jail. "He was about to start a one-man crime spree through Texas."

The next day I found myself returning to the sheriff's office with Grizzled Bill. But it wasn't so Bill could turn himself in. As it turned out, old Abernathy was looking for a deputy.

"You want me to be your deputy?" Grizzled Bill asked, not believing what he heard. "You have any idea who I am?"

"Sure I do," replied the sheriff.

There was dead silence. That's it, I thought, Bill's about to get thrown in jail. It was all a trick. The sheriff had trapped the uncatchable Bill into admitting who he was.

"You're a man of great aim," said the sheriff, to my astonishment. "And sound morality. And quick thinking. That makes you an ideal deputy—if you're willing, that is."

Grizzled Bill looked as if he'd been whacked in the head with a frying pan. "But you don't even know my name," said Grizzled Bill. "You should know that my name is …"

"Bill Hermitcrab," I interrupted, before he could say another word. "In all honesty, I don't think you could ask for a better deputy. Like you said, he's got all the qualities."

"Oh, so you know him, Sam?" asked the sheriff.

"Oh, yes," I said. "He's a man of character. One of the finest I know. And he just happens to be looking for a new job. So I wouldn't be at all surprised if he takes advantage of your kind offer." I turned to Grizzled Bill and gave him a look fraught with meaning.

"Oh," said Grizzled Bill. "Yes. Yes. I accept your offer."

"Hot diggity dog!" said Sheriff Abernathy. "This is great news!"

"It certainly is!" I agreed. I've never been so relieved. And that, believe it or not, is how one of Texas's most famous outlaws became one of its finest law enforcers.

Chapter 5
A Brand-New Bill

Sheriff Abernathy retired three years later. "Bill Hermitcrab" was immediately elected to fill his position. It was truly astounding. Bill had transformed himself from a man who committed robberies to a man who prevented them.

Two years later, I had finally saved up enough money and was ready to quit my job at the Triple J. I had been accepted at a college called Haverford, in Pennsylvania. I would be graduating with the class of 1874. There was, in fact, even more good news. Eloise and I were planning to be married the following May.

"That's wonderful news!" said Grizzled Bill—I mean Sheriff Bill Hermitcrab—when I told him.

"But there's more," I said. "Bill, I'd like you to be my best man."

"That's the nicest thing anyone's ever asked of me," he said, tears gleaming in the corners of his eyes. "Hey," he said to the few men lounging around in their cells. "Give my pal Sam a hand!" And they did.

What happened after that? After the wedding, Eloise and I moved to Pennsylvania, and I started taking classes. I also kept in contact with Bill through the mail. Turned out that Bill was still out to do some good for ordinary folk.

You see, in 1871, the Heiferville Town Council enacted some new ordinances. They were designed to protect the rights of the working man. No one thought anything would change, really. But they were wrong. As soon as these laws were passed, Bill went after mean old Mr. Wilkinson. He fined him for underpaying his men and overworking them. He even threw Wilkinson in jail overnight when he wouldn't help a man who'd been injured mending one of the ranch's fences.

I heard that Bill said to Wilkinson, "I ought to keep you locked up, so you can see how it feels. But I won't. Know why? I'm an honest man now, Wilk. More than I can say for you."

Wilkinson had to pay so much money in fines that Heiferville used this money to improve the town. It helped some poor families build better houses, fixed up the school, and built a hospital. I had to laugh. Old Bill had gotten Wilkinson after all.

* * * * *

    Eloise and I moved back to Heiferville years later. I became the town doctor. I'd missed the sunsets and the way the wind swept through the valleys. Eloise loved Texas too. And now, Bill was the mayor of Heiferville.

    One night, as my children played with his deck of cards, we sat down in Bill's parlor, sipping on tall, frosty glasses of lemonade. "So," I asked my old friend, "now what?"

    "Glad you asked," said Bill, with a grin. "See, Heiferville is the best town in all of Texas. We have a new school. Every child attends it."

    "And whatever happened to Old Wilkinson?" I asked.

    Bill chuckled. "Remember those men you worked all those fifteen-hour days with?"

    "How could I forget?"

    "Guess who owns the Triple J now?" he said with a wide grin. "Now I knew Wilkinson was weary of paying all those fines. But he just wasn't going to change. So I told him he had one choice. Give up the ranch and get the heck out of town. And he couldn't argue, because I'm the mayor!"

    "From outlaw to mayor," I said, raising my lemonade in a toast to Bill. "Seems perfectly natural to me."

A Brief History of Texas

In the beginning, Texas was not part of the United States. It was, in fact, a state within the Republic of Mexico. However, over the years, more and more settlers from the United States moved into Texas.

In October 1835, these settlers, along with Mexicans who lived in Texas, revolted against the Mexican government. On March 2, 1836, the Republic of Texas officially declared its independence.

On March 6, the famous Battle of the Alamo began in San Antonio. After a two-week siege, General Santa Anna and his Mexican forces overran the fort and killed the roughly 200 Texans defending it. But the Republic of Texas eventually secured its independence after defeating Mexico in the Battle of San Jacinto, on April 21.

In December 1845, Texas was annexed to the United States as the 28th state. But less than a year later, the Mexican-American War broke out. The war, which was partly caused by disputes over Texas's borders, was won by the United States in 1848.

Although Texas seceded from the Union in February 1861, it was re-admitted after the Civil War in 1870.

The Alamo, San Antonio, Texas